Healing is like Poetry

K Cropper

BookLeaf Publishing

Presentation by *BookLeaf Publishing*

Web: www.bookleafpub.com

E-mail: info@bookleafpub.com

ISBN: 9789357212427

First edition 2023

DEDICATION

To those I have, do and will love

Part One

I listened.
I waited.
I hoped.
I pleaded.
I questioned.
I reflected.
I implored.
I condemned.
I cried.
I broke.
I fought.

My Home

You destroyed my home
No, not literally
Typical me to use a metaphor
Typical you to choose to misunderstand it
You destroyed the home inside me
My safe place within myself
With your undignified rage
Unsolicited advice
Unjustified opinions
About the repairs I needed to make
You know? The ones you found
Oh, and the ones you created
Then you left
You told me my home is my responsibility
How could the damage be your fault!
And that I should never have let you in
If I wasn't willing to hear your feedback
You were perhaps right about one thing;
I should never have let you in

Twisted Compliments

You're so kind, you'd say, you're always thinking of others.
You're so kind, you'd say, you may as well be a door mat.

You're so warm, you'd say, you brighten up the whole room.
You're so warm, you'd say, you're just putting on a show.

You're so funny, you'd say, you are so quick and witty.
You're so funny, you'd say, but only I could understand your humour.

You're so beautiful, you'd say, you don't even know it.
You're so beautiful, you'd say, but not the most beautiful I've seen.

You're so interesting, you'd say, I love how your mind works.
You're so interesting, you'd say, your thinking is so warped.

You're so empathetic, you'd say, I feel like you 'get me'.
You're so empathetic, you'd say, but you only use it to manipulate.

You're so accomplished, you'd say, you work so hard.
You're so accomplished, you'd say, but I've done better.

You're so clever, you'd say, your intelligence is truly something.
You're so clever, you'd say, but not very smart, you're naïve.

You're so confusing, I'd say, but I want to understand.
You're so confusing, I'd say, but I never will.

Puzzle Pieces

A box of fragments
Designed to be made whole
You took each piece
You looked, you saw, you felt
You admired the intricacy
The concentration in your eyes
And at your fingertips
You completed it
And then broke it all apart
As you do
As is expected
But
You lost pieces
You took pieces
You swapped pieces
You kept pieces for yourself
So no one else
When they picked up that puzzle
Could ever solve it

Return to Sender

I neatly wrapped it up
The gift you asked for
To be sent to you
First class
Patterned paper and ribbons
Your favourite colours
With a handwritten note
I followed your directions
The perfect gift
You said
Hurry up and send it
You said
Yet
To my surprise
I found the gift back on my doorstep
Familiar, but bruised
The colours worn
The paper torn
Ribbons frayed
And as I took hold
Of the gift now unwanted
Gently in my hands
And asked why it was back
Why it was so damaged
You said

It was like that when you found it
When we both knew it wasn't
You said
This wasn't what I asked for
When we both knew it was
You said, finally
I changed my mind
Return to sender

The Queen Has Lost Her Crown

It unfolded like a movie
It always does with you
The dazzling dreams imparted
Perhaps too good to be true

The plot holes begin to emerge
As your storyline falls through
The hero becomes the villain
Conveniently rewritten by you

Your true character emerges
As your movie mask falls down
You unravel right before our eyes
The Queen has lost her crown

You scornfully direct the ending
Amongst chaos and confusion
Your audience sees the truth
The reality of your illusion

Part Two

I slept.
I read.
I wrote.
I painted.
I walked.
I ran.
I prayed.
I meditated.
I talked.
I connected.
I explored.
I learned.
I accepted.
I understood.
I forgave.
I released.
I let go.

Dreams

Dreams are funny old things
A concoction of memories
Mixed with hopes
Mixed with regrets
A wonderful place to escape
A scary inescapable place too
Restful
Or Restless
Sleep still comes
Dreams that soothe
Dreams that scare
Dreams that solve and repair

Words

At first
The words wouldn't come
I tried and tried
But there was nothing
Bar the blank page
The pen in my trembling hand
The tick of the clock
The sound of my heart thumping
And then
Not at all then all at once
The words came
Your words and my words
Tangled toxically together
Harsh imprints on the page
Anger, loss, betrayal
Haunting and hollow
So many words
So much confusion
Until my words began to stand out
Love, peace, hope
The ink brighter
The writing neater
The message clearer
Your words faded
Incomprehensible and irrational

Forgotten scribbles of nonsense
Written over a millions times now
You'd hardly know they'd ever existed

True Colours

Not all attacks
Require a response or a rise
Not all truths
Will be apparent from the lies
Not all intentions
Are clearly visible with your eyes
Not all villains
Will let down their disguise
Not all heartbreak
Will lead to your demise
People's true colours
Are often a surprise

Sit With Sadness

Sit with it
As it tumbles through your chest
Twists and turns in your tummy
Sit with it

Sit with it
As the tears swell in your eyes
Burning red hot on your face
Sit with it

Sit with it
As your thoughts run wild
Stories that ellicit more waves
Sit with it

Then

Sit with it
As you regain your breath
And the trembling subsides
Sit with it

Sit with it
As the tide goes out again
And you reconnect with yourself

Sit with it

Sit with it
As the storm has now passed
And your inner peace has been restored
And sit with that for a while

Finding Me

I needed to find the me I lost
So I searched for me anywhere and everywhere
In the autumn sunshine
In the colours of nature
In the beauty of light and dark
In the emotive nature of poetry
In the warm words of wisdom
In the unwavering support from my allies
In the wholesome hugs
In the songs that called out to be heard
In the smiles of strangers
In the synchronicities and signs
In the adventures I planned
In the learning of new things
In the movement of my body
In the mindful moments of self love
In the courage to look inwards

And there I was, I found me again

The strength in my softness
The compassion in my core
The loyalty of my love
The depth of my deliverance
Here, I am

Intuition

Connecting to you was difficult
I couldn't make out what you were saying
And if I did
I mistook you for Anxiety
She's often around too
I could feel you there
Guiding me in your own little way
Once I had quietened
Sat still and really listened
I realised you weren't my critic
Or an anxious thought
You were my saviour
You had always been

Part Three

I danced.
I sang.
I wondered.
I wandered.
I planned.
I dreamed.
I laughed.
I believed.
I expanded.
I strengthened.
I grew.
I healed.

Small Things Become Big

Perspective comes with healing
Beauty shows itself if you look closely.

Let the small things that make your heart smile,
Become big.

Perspective comes with healing
Beauty shows itself if you look closely.

Stars

Sometimes I look at the stars and think
Of the twinkle in your eye
How they all must have aligned to allow for 'us'
Tiny, magnificent sparks of light
But, more often now
They remind me of the space you created
Galaxies and universes of distance
And how sometimes
Things can be more beautiful from afar
For being too close to a star
It would swallow me up and burn me
Like your words
And how our eyes can deceive us
Along with our hearts
Because when you look closely
The glow of that star disappears

I Can Do Hard Things

I couldn't before but now I can
I can run until my legs ache
I can paint entire murals
I can read whole books in a day
I can learn a entirely new skill
I can meditate peacefully
I can forgive myself fully
I can set boundaries of solid stone
I can drag myself up from the ocean floor
I can swim for miles
I can see painful reminders and not flinch
I can see the truth you tried to hide
I can take care of myself
I can do hard things

Bravery

We judge our courage and bravery on the demons and dragons we have fought. The epic battles and the moments of fire, decimation and destruction. We ask ourselves how well we brandished our sword and stood sturdy with our shield. We forget the small battles it took to win the fight within ourselves. Getting out of bed that Wednesday morning. The call we made to a friend. The promises we kept. The moments we gave ourselves what we needed, not what we wanted. The tiniest of choices that entirely depended on our own courage within. There is bravery in every single choice you make for you. For you.

You Will Always Have Yourself

It's funny
That until you are broken by another
Loneliness
Creeps in like a cold draught in winter
You forget
That you always have one person with you
It's you
You are with you 100% of the time
Consistently
The relationship you have with yourself
Throughout time
Is the only true constant in your world
So why not
Make it the one that nourishes your soul
Has got your back
As you will always have yourself, no matter
what

Boundaries

I had built a stone wall
A moat containing sharks
Surrounding myself
Keeping the bad out
Keeping myself in

I added gateways
I replaced the stone with wood
I allowed some good in
I had missed the good
I allowed myself out

Boundaries are necessary
But over time they may change
Wood is lighter than stone
And just as effective

Healing is like Poetry

Sometimes your poem is
short, sweet, subtle.
The road to your healing too can be
Short, Sweet, Subtle.
What feels like a an epic ongoing journey...
is welcomed in a matter of moments.

Sometimes the words of your poem wander,
whirl and wind across the page, there is always
more to write, to express, to gather together.
The road to your healing may feel like this too
The mind will wander, whirl, and wind
Inescapable and exhausting
There's always more to feel, to express, to gather
together.
But you get there.

Sometimes only you will understand the words
on the page.
And this is okay.
Your poem, your healing, is yours.

Words weave their way through your body.

When you learn it is only you who can write
your own poem,
You also learn it is only you who can weave
your spirit back together.

I hope that you choose to weave the most
magical of words
Of kindness, love, courage, resilience, strength.
The bravery to honour your pain
Weaved in with the celebration of finding
yourself.

Write, write, write. Heal.
We are all rooting for you.

www.ingramcontent.com/pod-product-compliance
Lightning Source LLC
Chambersburg PA
CBHW051756130826
49812CB00033B/1181
9789357212427